THE WELL
Poems from Twin Pines Farm

THE WELL

Poems from Twin Pines Farm

written by

Nancy Huxtable Mohr

Dear Pat,
In gratitude for all
you do to preserve the
heritage of the land.
Best,
Nancy

BUTTERNUT PRESS

2018

All proceeds of *The Well: Poems from Twin Pines Farm*
will be donated to the Otsego Land Trust, a 501c3
in Otsego County, Cooperstown, New York.

Picture Credits

The Well emblem on title page by Robert Perry

Photography by Paul Kidder

Twin Pines Farm, Watercolor, 1980, and Millers Mills Free Baptist Church, Pen and Ink, 1980, by Robert Huxtable

Twin Pines Farm, Home of D. G. Young, Town of Columbia, Herkimer, New York, Lithograph, approximately 1860

Letters on section head pages: Elizabeth McKoon Young

For Kemet, Anna, and Jackson

TABLE OF CONTENTS

Prologue

Part 1

GRANDMOTHERS

Rhoba Williams McKoon

Elizabeth McKoon Young

Helen Young Huxtable

Hope Brown Huxtable

Part 2

TWIN PINES: 1940-2005
James and Adeline Weaver Huxtable

Part 2, Continued

POEMS FROM TWIN PINES FARM

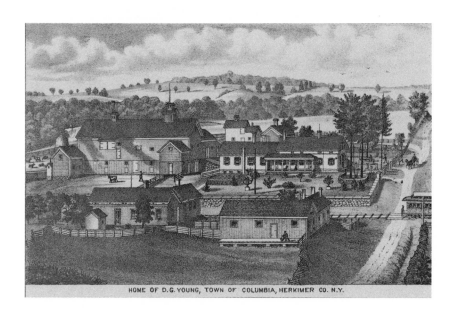

HOME OF D.G. YOUNG, TOWN OF COLUMBIA, HERKIMER CO. N.Y.

Prologue

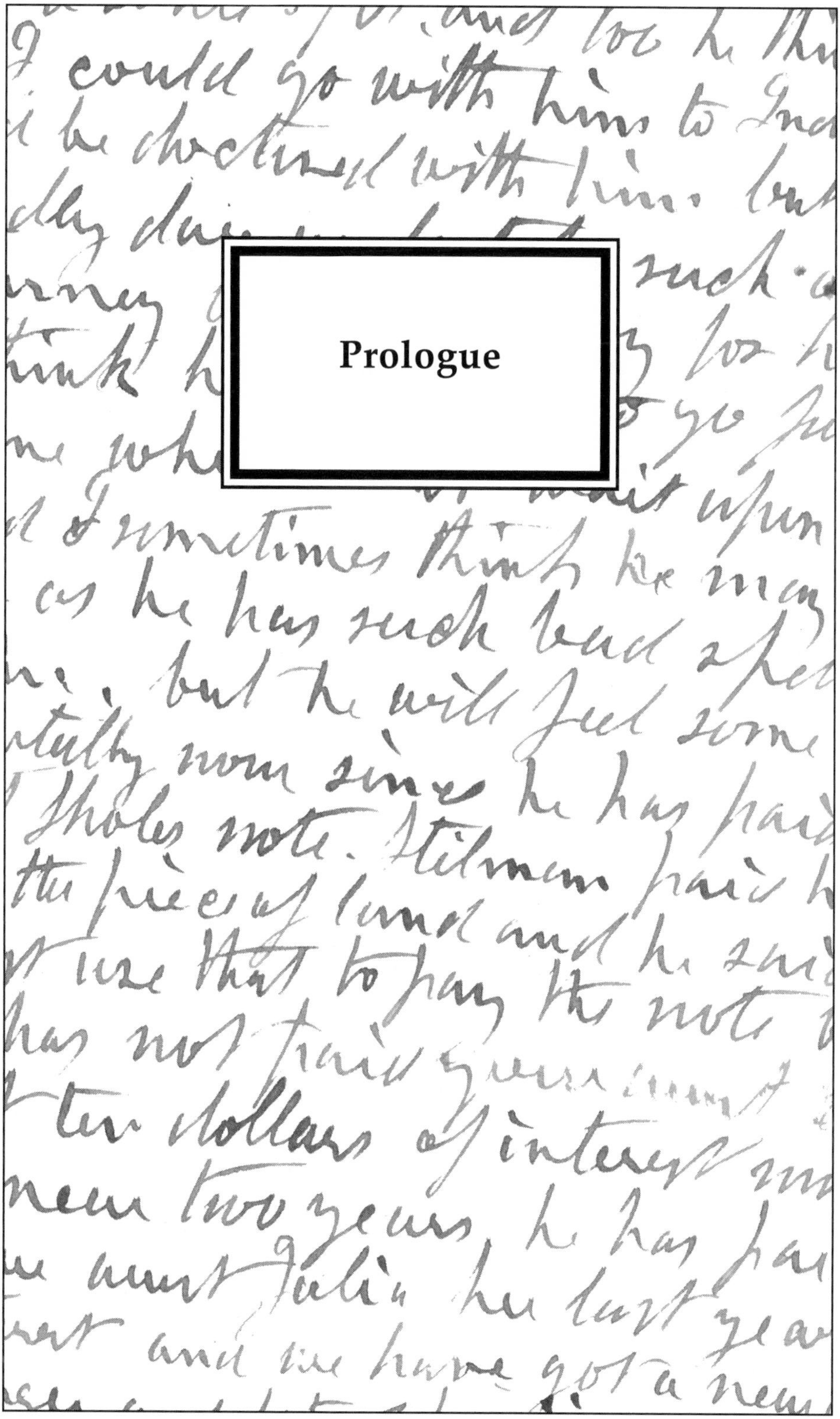

Words from a dipped pen
frayed diaries, yellow letters...

In The Attic

A pine trunk sits under cobwebs and mouse droppings. Words
from a dipped pen, frayed diaries, yellowed letters—lines written
over lines to save paper. Old words: *strop, the privy, pickets, pie
plant*. A cross stitched cloth under the lid keeps the silence clean.

I never think of them without their flesh—Helen's clouded eyes,
a daughter's diseased leg buried under the rose bush, or sharp
ribs at the end of a long winter. I pick field stone or walk beside
Rhoba, or work in a hot kitchen making food for men in the field.

But who dug the well for the cabin? Who watched the 1860
eclipse while D.G. boiled sap? Who listened to Grandpa James'
sermons sweeping earth of sin or folded Floyd's bullet ridden
uniform? What did Aunt Laura write to Eleanor Roosevelt?

Sometimes, I stand watching my grandmothers' lives like a
midwife in the borning room. But the silence is never silent. At
times I hear the strangest noise—as if the dead could clap. Then,
I breathe and listen to a branch brush the dormer pane.

Lifting My Granddaughter To The Well

A soft fold over the edge, pink shoes lifted,
her image buoyant in the water below.
She stares into the cylindrical dark,
past moss and mottled snails pulled back
in their casings. Her face disappears
in the bucket splash.

There and then not.

Now the earth's sweet liquid brims,
spills and falls back on the grass,
circles through roots to the well,
the river, and the bass pond.

Part 1

GRANDMOTHERS

Rhoba Williams McKoon
1771-1868

Elizabeth McKoon Young
1816-1891

Helen Young Huxtable
1845-1938

Hope Brown Huxtable
1887-1927

*I have prayed for this and then
regretted praying. This new life
will be a blessing and a curse —
something unstoppable.*

Rhoba Williams McKoon
1771–1868

Sixth descendant of Roger Williams. Married Martin
McKoon on October 25, 1789. In 1795, they walked from
Rhode Island by ox cart with two children to the New
York wilderness, built a log cabin, and hand dug a well.
They had 15 children, 11 of whom lived. She was the local midwife. In 1807, they built a farmhouse. Her mother
died when she was four. Her father lived to 100 and was a
chaplain in Washington's Army at Valley Forge. Two sons
and four grandsons fought in the Civil War. She died at 97
at Twin Pines and is buried in the local churchyard.

She Did What She Could
[Rhoba Williams McKoon's headstone]

Move me, wheel,
from the sea, by the Hudson,
through woods, fields.

My hand on your rim.
Growling bellies, oxen smells.
Make my feet go with my prayers.

Have I brought what I need
for the world ahead?
Who will ask for my stories?

Will I find my Snakeroot and Sweet Ciceley?
Will the peonies survive?
Will I find good dirt, water for a well?

15

Talking To My Peonies

Remember how dirt feels
and warm muck on your stems.
Roots expanding. Your first buds—
pale, then deep pink and crimson.

Think of the thunder and the rain
waiting as I walk beside you.
No sound from the stones
but the sun will be hot by summer.

I have prayed for this and then
regretted praying. This new life
will be a blessing and a curse—
something unstoppable.

When the snow descends, don't blame
me, the woman who insisted you had
to come and survive too. I know God
is walking us both along this weedy path.

After A Long Walk From Rhode Island

The sound of sea in me is gone.
I hope I never eat another possum.
My feet hard as leather. Bone tired.

I could fling open my arms,
grab this soil, this solitude, a spring sky.
The Mohawks call it Unadilla.

Deep woods, a strong brook, earth ready.
What possessed me to bring peonies?
But here comes a feathered shoot.

First Days

All the plain hard talk—how
we were starved for land.

Forget the ox cart—a raft where
we discovered nothing.

I am numb from hauling water
while the men dig a well.

God, have You been listening,
especially here?

Sweet James

Tomorrow I'll pick stone, set my mind right.

My nipples already hard, his milk gone
and the bruise of suckling. Our bed
empty. He was a fern barely unfurled.

Sun on his coffin, his grave dirt smells
like a harrowed field. A split in the wood—
I almost see my boy under his small quilt.

The air's full of wings and chimes
of the church bell. I must get busy—stones,
a batch of johnnie cakes, a walk to the well.

Sabbath

But who can sit all day. Satan himself is on the run.
    Rhoba Williams, 1798

Smoke and sweetness, kettle on a slow boil—
the perfect time to layer lard. A new heartbeat
in my belly. Festus said spring would come
and now so many new brooks feeding
our well. The peepers out at dusk.
I seem to know what they know—
there is no twig of me not trembling with joy.

.

Dearest Sister Mercy

Your words through mine.
I could be by the bay talking to you.
Last night, the baby's cries and cough
reached all the way to Martin
in the barn. We never slept.
Who would guess at our life now?
Already we are naming the fields.
Two babies buried and another coming.
Neither of us could see the cost of this.
A small mistake or the wrong weather
and we are finished. Rain coming hard.
Your black kettle boils. The well is full.
I can hear Martin coming for his meal.

Rhoba Finds A Bear In Her Cabin

This morning—sod spun earth, a green
and singing space with pure air to drink.
Yesterday, the black clouds like a chest of fur.

Down at the creek, holes in the thick ice
where something, but nobody, fell.
Some movement in the cabin.

My arms still shake after his exit—
the panting giant, swing my broom,
shout to Martin to save the cows.

Run. Yell to the children to hide.
Breathe as if I am finished and
Satan himself is after me.

In and out the house all day, watch
the trees, look for his return.
Tonight, a moon claws the dark.

Dear Brother Freelove

Silence
on the hills. Fall air
through the windows
in the borning room.
Baby Helen's cries
fill the house.
She arrived
in the shape of a human,
small and sweet.
She's missing three fingers
but this is how
God will find her.

After Martin

What if we had never married and
you had notched a life beside the sea?

This month of leaf and mud, rain fills
the barnyard, your burial spot, the well.

You were worked out. Hands always
on the plow, the seed bags, the cows.

I look to the hills. Listen!
Wind in old woods you knew by heart.

One By One

I think these diseases arise from a lack of pluck.
    Rhoba in a letter to her sister Mercy, 1862

One by one, they leave, whistling.
Five loads of soldiers left for camp
at Mohawk today to be mustered,
I can not speak without crying
and so I stayed home.

More news of the bloody fight.
Terrible exposure. Dysentery.
I am afraid to open letters.
Many plead they are ill
and can't enlist. They will not bleed.

God, Field, And Fire

This is my last letter to you my last child.
    Rhoba to Elizabeth, 1868

Carmi took me down to the creek this morning.
I could feel the frost cut through my shoes.
Chunks of ice floated past our bucket.
Now is late and the logs fail to light
A neighbor writes this. I am too feeble.

Be strong, strong, Elizabeth. At your center, keep God
who has been here since we began our new life.
He is in the fire, the field, your hands.
Fill the family pew on Sundays.

Pay no heed when I am gone,
                for what we live comes back to us.

Beginning

Something in me wants
to walk again from Providence
with them—living, dead,
and unborn. Their lives wound
tightly in me. Now they are names
in our Bible. Some birthed
in snowstorms, others
in spring thaw or born on Thursday
so I could plant corn on Friday.

Please, God. Leave
a trace. How careful
I have been not to picture
war. Now all I can see.

Elizabeth McKoon Young
1816–1891

Fifteenth child of Martin and Rhoba McKoon. Married local farmer and inventor, David Golden (D.G.) Young, October 14, 1841. They had two children Floyd and Helen. Floyd died in the Civil War on June 5, 1861. Elizabeth was active in the Abolitionist movement and ran the farm during her husband's frequent absences selling his inventions. In 1882, they traveled to California by train to visit relatives. She wrote a poem for their 50th wedding anniversary in 1891. They both died within the year and are buried in the churchyard.

War Talk

Our boys are cold in the fields. No bandages
or medicine. Hard tack, rancid water, and dysentery.
    Elizabeth in a letter to Cousin Sophie, 1861

Tomorrow, David leaves for Albany
for the train south. We sit tense across
the table. Johnnycakes and syrup between us.
Onions frying hard. How I weep with them.
Mother's fingers roll dough and drop sugary
balls in lard. But sweet smells don't decrease
the talk of guns and Lincoln's generals.
Our boy molds in his tent, cooks mice.
I am sick of gunshot. Target practice
in the woods while the maples shudder.

Prayer

Floyd Young, Wounded
New York World, newspaper. May 28, 1861

A hole in him, blood.
Still living, breathing,
among the thousands
on the fields? Silence.

Please, God. Leave
a trace. How careful
I have been not to picture
war. Now all I can see.

The Ache Of Everything

I must write how it was—
      how straight he walked down the road
      with his new canteen and musket.

His letters of boredom, rot, a bloodied
creek. His father brought him back in a pickle barrel.
My only son—we needed him home.

Outside, chimney smoke fades in the early hours—
    my stropped heart by the well and wormed fence
    with the ache of everything.

Thunder starts. Time will come when I can sleep.
Blessed rain but so little erased with the rush and suck of water.

Mother

Mother is still with us—but how long?
    Elizabeth to her cousin Sophie about her mother
    Rhoba, January 1868

War, mud, cold, hunger, blood.
She wore brown clothing, ate spongey potatoes,
foraged woods for pie plant and cowslips.
Dug a well, chased a bear from our cabin.

She called on God Almighty for help with
our coughs and winter wheat. Yelled at
Satan over the dead cow and war.
I hope her peonies will bloom again this spring.

Looking Out After The Blizzard

The pond is a sheet of glass. Black and white earth.
    Elizabeth in her diary, February 1883

Strange shapes covered in snow—
outlines, angles at odds with everything.
I think that must be the rain barrel, the well,
Deacon's old sawhorse. Everything light
and shadow. The glint of ice on the far meadow.

Above the world there is only blue, blue everywhere.
I dreamt last night of a walk in the orchard rows,
with the peepers' chirp. Our creek leaping
the road. But now is the hard almanac of winter.
Now is cider sauce and melting snow in pails.

On The Train To California

Almond blossoms in winter
> Elizabeth in her letter home from
> their train trip to California, March 1882

I wade into grass to
wear the green like a skirt.
Through the train
window, cloudless skies
and fields with no stones.
No snow banks only
white blooms adrift on dirt.
We can't be heard over
churning wheels. Only clasped,
callused hands forgetting pails.

Mud, Mud, Mud
[Elizabeth in her diary, March 1884]

Dark, dark. Mud, mud in every crack,
clumps on the floor boards.
A cold day dragging to its cold end.

No one passes on the road—already noon.
Three times, the sun has tried to shine and failed.
Wash waits in tubs, chamber pots are full.

Yesterday, we had one rider. I heard the horse
grunting up the hill, rushed to the window—
too late. Was it the pastor saving souls?

Communion

Your father said Communion. 60 in church.
The sap is running.
    Elizabeth's letter to her daughter Helen,
    March 1887

1.

Look, I tell myself. I tell my soul,
the maples are ready with their sap.
I hear the tin pings of drips hitting
buckets from my pew. Then James' voice—

This is my body given for you. Here is the cup.

I can almost taste the first spoonful
of syrup on fresh snow, sweet steam
from the sap house. There is nothing evil
in church, just truth waits on the outside.

Take this in remembrance of me. Amen.

2.

Finally back in homespun and boots.
I lift my eyes to the hills from whence cometh my help.
Finally, great gulps of air, slow walks
past trees, passing the collections along the line.

Again, I tell myself, here is forgiveness.
These maples stand like saints in stained glass.
The light unravels on the path before me.
Standing here, Lord, I am ready for anything.

Air And Reason

I must try not to let my feelings rise above my reason.
If I did, I should think I might not live long.
    Elizabeth's letter to her daughter Helen, 1889

Sifted yolks, smell of burned
feathers, six hens plucked and in
their prisons. Cider worked enough.
Sun swirling on the laundry line.

What are we doing, we two alone?
We pick stone year after year,
bake as if the house were full?
Floyd gone, a phantom limb.

The names in this house will
change and ours will move
to the churchyard. Fingers
will rub my headstone.

But I give myself a good lungful
of October air and reason,
write this letter with what light
is left in one last stub of candle

That's all I know. God help us.

Winter Coming

I dreamed of sweet Laura in my arms
and it makes me want to see her.
I can hardly keep the tears back.
    Elizabeth to her daughter Helen, after she
    left Twin Pines with grandchildren to return
    to Boston, November 1899

Storms coming but the tubs
are full—one wash, the other butter
for you on the next train. Tell
the children, I baked pies—-three
mince, three apple, and a turnover—
fried a pan of cakes, 65 sugar cookies,
and bread rising for tomorrow.
We took the cider barrel to the cellar,
just worked enough to be good.
I watched the children sitting straight
backed on the train. Let them go.

Barnstable, London, France
War is coming.
Dark signs—chaos at the train station,
troops in the street, the same tears.

Helen Young Huxtable
1845–1938

Second child of D.G. and Elizabeth Young. Helen was born with severe hearing loss and only two fingers on her left hand. She was 16 when her brother Floyd was killed in the Civil War. She married James Huxtable, immigrant from England and Baptist minister, in 1873. They lived in various New England locations and summered at Twin Pines. James became an ardent follower of Charles Darwin, was ostracized from the church, and became a Unitarian minister. Helen ran the farm after her parents died while James spent much of his time in Boston. They returned to England for a summer in 1914 when she was 59. They had four children: Florence, Darwin, Arthur, and Laura. Their daughter Florence died of pneumonia in 1924. James died in 1929 and is buried in Boston. Helen is buried at Twin Pines.

Hunger

Oh, for apples, fried cake, pies and cheese.
    Helen's letter to her mother from Whitestown
    Academy, March 1863

Dear Mama,

Only bread, butter and applesauce for dinner here.

Last night I got six cookies for three cents.

Soon we will be about starved.

I could eat a bushel of apples if I were home.

Saturday and Sunday are the longest days.

I can never stay here five more weeks.

Bring me medicine for my hearing.

I am so tired of living here.

I can picture you at the window where you stand.

Five o'clock. I hear the bell for dinner.

Gravity

It was a beautiful morning.
How can I live without my Florence?
  The entry from Helen's journal, March 21, 1924,
  the day her daughter Florence died.

The sky was grey flannel.
Twigs and a sparrow rushed
along by the brilliant gale.

From the outside,
I was the figure crouched
over a bed holding a dove.

Her breath burned red in the room.
Her end was as bright
and new as feathered gold.

Then, I was the woman unable to stand.

Moving

Groan, another move.
   Helen's journal, March 1925

Each room empties with silence,
escapes without a moan
into the trunks. O, let these things—
Lincoln's picture, Mother's cut glass—
recede from my feet like an outgoing
tide. I am slow as time. My bones
like a bleached carcass found
in spring woods. I am dry tinder
to his anger but move we must.
Charles Darwin never dreamt what
troubles he caused with his believers.

The Devil

Woodchuck again for dinner.
      Helen in her journal, 1927

I hope this one's the devil
who's been digging
underneath the porch.
Tsk. Tsk.
God, forgive my evil chuckle
when they brought it to my kitchen.
Dark and delicious.

Tiny Bird

Goodbye, London. On deck to see a gorgeous rainbow on the water. At sunset, a tiny bird landed on my left, then to my feet, then off it flew content.

> Helen from her diary on the ship from London
> to Boston, September 1914

Now in the Universe, there is a hole.
The churches will be filled. Tears.
Another war to endure. The poets will
have more to say of death and little joy.

Now back to farm life. Trees turning
and green lawn starting to brown.
The smell of animals and wood fires.
Wash to be done. Chamber pots to empty.

Sea spray and white foam.
From here, the ocean looks calm
stretching all the way to England.
O, to fly away with this tiny bird.

Words From Her Journal

1897

How many times have I been on this trip—
Boston to farm and back?
Mother and Father waiting.
The old walls waiting. That first sip
from the well or maybe still some cider.

1903

1.
Grandson Richard does not forget to cry
but I am content to be deaf.
He is unharmed by the world. A blank slate.
My arms ache and together we breathe.
I cook soup, wash diapers, rock happy.

2.
This soaker means to wake me
but nothing will move me in my bed tonight.
O, back, unbend and rest. So many mouths to feed.
Tomatoes, beans, squash in today. More tomorrow.
The peepers drown in thunder.

3.
Last dip of water from the well.
A fine ride in the new carriage.
Last carrots pulled before the frost.
Goodbye, old walls.

4.
Evening's come. Santa was too generous.
I said, Take them back—all but the paper,
diaries and the fine nibbed pen.
What would Mother say of this excess?

1908

1.
Sun burned faces and empty stomachs.
Eggs to collect. Hay to mow.
More beds in the Cheese House.
I am half used up.
What was it I said to the well?
You must be careful not to disappear.

2.
Oh, the quiet and the clean. Everyone gone.
A good nap in the rocking chair,
no flies, no men.

1914

1.
Barnstable, London, France
War is coming.
Dark signs—chaos at the train station,
troops in the street, the same tears.

2.
I must admit, Valentino was, by himself,
worthy of the trip, cost and hour spent.
But moving pictures? So much is a waste
these days—telephones, autos, wringers,
except for my sewing machine.

1930

1.

      I lift up mine eyes unto the hills.
But, my eyes so weak, I must keep memorizing
Tennyson and Psalms to start the day.
      In looking on the happy autumn fields,
      and thinking of the days that are no more.

Much left to do.
      Time, a maniac scattering dust,
      and Life, A fury slinging flame.

Tsk, Tsk. Feeling sorry for myself again.

2.
I swore when I was 90, I'd fly in a plane.
If you can live with a man for over 50 years,
you can trust another one will put you
in the heavens and bring you back to earth again.

3.
Everything now is Just Right.
Useless to complain. Especially now:
James is gone. I am surrounded by children.

What I am certain of tonight
curled under Arthur's snores:
      let it happen whatever is next
      let there be life and death.

Hope Brown Huxtable

1887–1927

Hope Brown married Arthur Huxtable, third child of James and Helen Huxtable, on January 10, 1911. She was raised in Ipswich, Massachusetts. They moved to Twin Pines when Arthur took over the farm from his parents James and Helen. For some time, they had to live in the Cheese House with no running water. They had three sons: Arthur, Henry, and James. She died from surgery complications at age 40 and is buried in the family cemetery in Ipswich.

The Dancing Season

*I went out and danced until 1:30 am—and I love to dance. Had
more fun. Then went to bed with no Precious to cuddle up to—*
    Hope in a letter to her husband Arthur, June 1911

June, at last, and the Grange gave a party.

In my sleep, I asked you to let me go dancing.
I said to myself:
        one week more and he will be home.

I left the hearthstone and the laundry,
        mayflies,
        water to be drawn.
I left the whey draining in the sink.

I know the look of you beside me on our bed
but I could not miss a dancing party and be home alone.

Certainty

My dear Father and Mother Huxtable, I would by far
rather go through an operation, even though a serious
one, than to drag around as some miserable thing for years.
    Hope to her in-laws James and Helen,
    August 1923

Because I was bed-bound all morning,
the windows covered, I drew
outlines on the bed-sheets
with my fingertips. Wrote letters.
I could hear the men draw
the second cutting, Maude worked
the old wringer, telling the boys
to keep the noise down near the stairs.

What I am certain of tonight
curled under Arthur's snores:
      let it happen whatever is next
      let there be life and death.

Part 2

TWIN PINES: 1940–2000

Tails slap, wings against weather,
the sheen of sky on water.

You must have known then — days, years,
would disappear in a haze of hard work.
You would set your table with zinnias ...

James Huxtable   Adeline Weaver Huxtable
1916–1999   1917–2005

My father James Huxtable, third son of Arthur and Hope Huxtable, married Adeline Weaver Huxtable in 1938 after both graduated from Cornell University. They lived in Ithaca where he taught at Cornell for two years and then moved back to the family dairy farm, Twin Pines, in 1940. Adeline worked as a social worker, librarian, and a farm wife. In addition to farming, James was a teacher for 30 years and New York State Assemblyman. Republican, of course. They had five children: Susan, Nancy, Deborah, Jon, and Rebecca Hope, several foster children, foreign exchange students, and eight grandchildren. Their son Jon died in a farm accident in 1983. Twin Pines, now a non-working farm, was sold to a cousin in 2000 and most of the land put into a land trust.

Twin Pines Farmhouse: 1940

You stepped into the dark kitchen
then realized the mound in the middle
of the floor was a heap of cold ash.

The house forgotten, stripped clean
including the wood stove. At least
they left the ash to tell you where to cook.

You must have known then—days, years,
would disappear in a haze of hard work.
You would set your table with zinnias,

candles, and cloth napkins—though flies
feasted on a day's dinner. The rooms
washed in rose and daisy wallpapers.

You breathed walls and floorboards back to life.
Dared to imagine beauty.
Spent hours weeding to find light inside peonies.

Sometime after, a field would be named for you
where on a summer day you drove a tractor topless.
But this house would never be called Adeline's.

Just your years of prayer, sweat, singing,
and admonition to your daughters:
        Never marry a farmer.

To Survive There Was No Small Feat

A toddler finds her way
out the farmhouse door, looking
for the horse who pulls wagons.
The sun fixed overhead.
Bob, the hired man ferries hay
from field to barn. He trusts the sky.

He fails to see her in the furrow
of her father's field, freshly plowed.
The wheel of his empty wagon going
forward precisely over the top
of the mounds and over her body
like a seed planted in fertile soil.
There, a speck. But it turns
in the corner of his eye. A change
in the light. A cry.

A few tears. Dirt falls
from gnarled fingers as he checks her.
Yet, only a small fragment of rib
sticks strangely from her chest.
Bob's voice—
I'm sorry. I'm sorry. I didn't see her.
in that crestfallen way one is sorry
for not catching a fledging in first flight.

She still sees old Bob at funerals,
gas stations, the feed store.
Always flustered, he bellows:
How ya doin' after I ran over ya?
Strange how her hand goes quickly to her chest.

The Second Child

My warm, wet hand in the calf's mouth
and she sucks, feeding on my fingers.
After chores I hide in a favorite tree to see
      how the sun will dent the sky,
        how Nancy Drew will solve her mystery,
        how long it takes my mother to find me.

This sweet maple's my small church,
a pew in a high crease of branches.
Barn swallows   orioles   bobolinks
        How do they know when it's safe to go home?

Ten Below

Clear sky, ten below,
Christmas coming.
We pile in a hay wagon,
tucked and wrapped,
ready for the ritual tramp
through deep snow.

This year's designated
tree waits for us. White
breath against white snow.
Listen to us, our young voices
so trusting. His callused hands
on the axe. We know those hands—
the hands that hold us.

Photo Of A Farm Girl Of The Fifties

Summer flicks specks
of light and shadow
along the milk house steps.
Two flimsy mounds point
under my flowered blouse,
legs like thin branches,
bones already vibrating.
A robin could build a home
in my nest of hair.

A vortex of Holsteins behind
me in the East Meadow—
a whole herd wound round
a maple's shadow in the heat.
A granite hedgerow rims
the field in black and white.
Strands of color come later,
woven like the fence line.

Millers Mills Ice Harvest

On Little Unadilla, men mark
and saw patterns, lift ice blocks
with tongs to wooden sleds.

A Clydesdale stands with steam
rising off his flanks, nudges my hand
with his wet nose. His driver flashes
black teeth and a winter belly
for my camera. His boots sunk in slush.

While water waits
for summer under our feet.

Girl With No Answer

Amber Whites and Plymouth Rocks:
I feed them early each morning.
Proud mother to chicks turned plump.

In the rain-fed fields, horseflies
are iridescent green. I carry my hens
around the farm, make introductions
to visitors, confess to them the secrets
of a twelve year old. Write hen-poems.

Trees bloom all through me
and there is no one else to tell.
Days are slow, are slow, are slow.

In mid-September, a man comes to twist
their necks. Jeweled heads dangle
at their breasts as they race through the yard.
Then, tossed in a feathered pile in a rusted truck.
He shakes my dad's hand. Never looks at me.

I didn't know the world was so blurred,
burnt. *It's a good lesson*, my parents say.
Green God, in your language of silence, tell me.

The East End
For Sue

Far east end of the house, next to the attic
and its trunks of treasure, long hall to our parents,
three siblings and two hired men in between.

Light and dark entered our room first.
Spring rains through cracks in windows,
snow inside sills in winter. Legions of wasps.

We quarreled over quilts in a heatless room,
curled like kittens for warmth, heard secrets
and worries of adults through a stove vent.

We shared measles, chicken pox, mumps.
We locked arms on Christmas morning
and bolted down the stairs together.

Sometimes we hung a sheet between teenage
territories, fought over the only white blouse.
The room's clarity still sticks in my head
like burdock burs. I draw it in my sleep.

Fresh Corn At Midnight

The corn's just ripe. Mom boils water
in the metal pot while we grab buckets
and walk to Dad's cornfield to rows
of Silver Queen. Delicious even raw.

Thoughts of buttered corn drip
and smear across the night
and silky laughter falls like
husks around our feet.

The Borning Room

Evening perhaps. Midwife with
towels ready on the four poster.
The husband waits in the barn
or kitchen for the squeal.
Then, the baby swathed in flannelled
light while the mother recovers from a
last push through open thighs.
Then the flow of pomegranate placenta.

Births were near windows—frost
squiggled or open to summer clouds.
So many mothers with children
at their breasts in this room,
red quilt from the cedar bride box
around their shoulders.

New Year's Eve 1958

A blaze in a field stone fireplace,
roads a testament of ice, cows loud
from the barn, parents in the kitchen.
Pastor Elliott gathers our youth group,
mostly cousins and sisters. We have
our teenage secrets but must write them
on paper and throw them in the fire.
Pastor Elliott is certain about everything.
What's right, wrong, black, white.
An old lion who can smell fear
and juicy teenage sin. He wants us
to trust Jesus. Beg His forgiveness.
Never mind whiskey passed in the kitchen
or *Goddammits* while lighting the fire.

Pyromaniac

I tried to be a good girl—
        deciphered the smell and syntax of boys
        their eyes fixed on my tight sweater.
I thought of
        Brando's chest in a tight shirt
        Elvis's hips swiveling
I wanted my breasts to ignite those boys
        like a pyromaniac burning down houses.

Mother's Day

Soft sleepy edges of Sunday morning;
sounds of the beating of egg whites
and pounding of a rolling pin in the kitchen
carry up the stairs. The perfume of lemon
and baking pie crust fill our farm house.

By the time I'm dressed in church clothes
the lemon pie is cooling at a slant
on the counter. Mountains of meringue are
perfectly hemmed by a rib of larded crust.
Mother allows me a moment's worship

before telling me to hurry, and get in
the Rambler. We must be on time to
              charge our Christian batteries.
She is ravenous for God but from the first hymn
to the last Lord's Prayer, I am ravenous for pie.

She wants to be remembered as good
wife and mother. Cookies for neighbors.
Flowers for church. Rooting for the Mets.
But today, she frowns as she puts the pie
on our table and says—
              Not my best.

Aunt Maude

       was ghostlike on summer visits to the farm,
read poetry as we played games around her feet.
Jaw perched above a tight collar, white hair in a bun,
dress like a milky shroud. Her translucent fingers
always held a book. She would command the front lawn
for most of the day and moved in breathless quiet.

Even while hanging sheets or feeding a child,
she would murmur: *a certain slant of light* or *peace
comes dropping slow*. Frost would flow from her
upstairs room at night. Over years, from her Boston
accent beneath the maple tree, amid the tractor noise
and cow moos, a figured stillness. A new language.

Bathroom Blues

Half past seven and four girls
hurry through the bathroom
to ready for the school day.

Dad races in from the barn
and claims his turn. He needs
a transformation: farmer to teacher.

Poor guy. Someone used
his razor to shave their legs.
No more hot water. No towels.

Problems with cows, hired men,
papers to grade and teenage girls
complaining they need more time.

Poor frazzled guy. Never mind.
Someday, he'll rest with *Reader's
Digest* while toileted in total silence.

Wind Still Blowing Through Him

To come in from the barn,
packed in the eye of a blizzard,
his hands grip ropes. He fights
            a white wind
no stopping, eyes closed, hand over hand.

Inside the house, Dad takes whiskey.
Lots of whiskey. Jiggers straight.
Wind still blowing through him,
            the whole of him
thanks the ropes. Slowly
he sinks into the sofa. No one talks.

Then, high laughter rushes out,
            wind driven
or whiskey driven. Overlapping laughter,
like another aspect of nature,
            like breaking waves.

Hours pass. Trees twist hard,
Slapped and shrouded. Finally still.
Our mailbox hangs high from a tree
            like a white dove.

The Slaughter Season

Dawn-lit paths are dangerous
as hairy-fingered triggers squeeze
bullets. Prints of talon, hoof, paw
show shadowy escapes. I hear
the breath of living beasts.

Autumn's harvest of blood.
Birds recircle to find a familiar
pond between rifle shots. Deer
antlers point skyward, sweep
a maple's branch off a pickup's roof.

I believe someone once stood
in the barn by tallow light, stripped
skin from a buck, hung the meat,
salted, and stored for winter.
Women washed off blood at the well.

Weed Pulling

Curved back, bent head, her hands pull
burdocks, dandelion, and goutweed.
She frees the peonies, hostas, and geraniums.
Twilight strains her eyes but she works
like a nun picking at a rosary.

Wild kids, hungry men, wet sheets, dirty pots,
but outside the house, the light is laid
across the stone wall, across the grass,
pulling the day back down where she works
next to quiet shadows, indisputably green.

Dryin' Days

You can always judge a woman by how she hangs her wash.
    Adeline to her daughters

Finally, a good *dryin' day*
when a morning breeze blows
and mother stands in the yard
with a basket full of sheets.
They tremble when first hung
and then balloon like white
sails on an open sea. She smiles.

The wooden pins stand at attention
and march along the laundry line,
next to the line of a railroad track,
and next to that, the line of a dirt road.
She goes to watch at her kitchen sink
while cars slow down, and heads turn
to see her sheets straight in the sunlight.

Feminine Geometry

Sisters remember the rescue of drowning
cats, Sunday train, ironing the family
tablecloth for Thanksgiving, sleigh rides
on Christmas—all remembered with different
authority. Birth order and farm chaos shrank
and aligned us until we formed our own feminine
geometry. Individual angles on a spring day.
Bodies, hearts, brains beat against each other
with multiple meanings in the same green
shuttered, clapboard farmhouse.

Gladiolas

Nobody sees a flower. Really, it is so small.
We haven't time and to see takes time
like to have a friend takes time.
   Georgia O'Keefe

Mom is on her way to church
before the pastor. Her arms
spread with garden gladiolas.
A buttered sun warms a spot
of driveway. Worry doesn't
show around her eyes.
She talks of tomatoes, melons,
August moons while back patio
laughter hangs in the air.
No one notices my work.
No. People do see your work.
Really. They are friends.

Fly Away Home
For Rebecca

Solitude ripples the pond,
      May becomes June.
Swarms of ladybugs, orbits
of vermillion, drift in
the opulence of air. This place
the beavers, not humans,
have mastered. Abandoned
hedgerows and meadows.

I think of the tenderness in this world
when someone shares your sorrow:
      your house is on fire
      your children are gone.

The dotted masses billow and float
toward the maple woods:
      Fly away. Fly away home.

Two Bowls

This will be my epitaph—sixty three years in the kitchen.
   Adeline's lament

In one bowl: grief.
In another: mounds of strength.
Shoulders hunched.
Hands scrape corn from cobs.

Egg cakes on breakfast plates,
while she cans the Bartlett pears,
picks, and shells peas.
Ready for months of winter.

No picnics on a warm beach,
ocean waves, no empty days.
Just steam from the pressure
cooker and tomatoes in the sink.

Wedding Day

She stood in socks and organza
on the oak stool, made slow circles.
Her mother knelt on the floor
and finished the hem. A phantom
bride in early morning before
the processional, the pin cushion
like a bouquet. A blank still
for her name on the license.

Now, relatives gather ferns
in the woods to decorate the church.
Women are baking hams and ziti
casseroles. Milking is finished.
Somewhere, the groom drinks a beer.
Soon, the church fills with people
wearing their good clothes.

But we should think of her, circling,
her dress unfinished. Her mother
kneeling beneath her. Their silence.

Beaver Pond

Apple tree growth and neglect,
leaf hemlines of burnt orange,

poplars like a heronry,
long legs stuck in the mud.

Jon's grave on the bank.
September winds float

a hermit canoe,
a last wedge of pearled light.

Granite hedgerows
in geometric fields.

Tails slap, wings against weather,
the sheen of sky on water.

Beyond Fingertips

Words, this morning, are just beyond my fingertips.
    Nancy in a letter to her mother, September 1966

One and one and one. Each dried pea
falls from my fingertips into a narrow row.
I push their tiny bodies deeper into the dirt,
a little cavern. Water from the hose or rain
and pea shoots emerge. Thousands
with a single purpose—a search for light.

But night after night, I drop words on the page
and they find no fertile ground. By morning,
I have killed them all. Dropped them down the well.
I work with tears and even the full moon—
but nothing. My fingertips put my poems
in little graves, hidden from the hot sun's sugar.

Worry

Worrying never stops. Why is it never on the list
of why not to have children?
    Adeline in a letter to daughter Nancy, September 1993

Her back was broken by worry. The walls
of her private room so choked with questions
on sleepless nights:
        the farm, Jim's health, no money, no sons
        children in creeks, trees, on barn roofs
        how many cows to sell for college, weddings.

And each morning, there began a tiny song trying to turn to praise.
Faith came with a small evidence of things.

And still now, grandchildren in a mixed-up world, in a rush
        to end their brief childhoods.
But tonight, a new moon leaps over the paint brushed hills—
        she looks to them for her help.

Big Blue

Dad sails his tractor over fields
as if it has guns on deck.
No conversation over the roar.

I grip my seat while he drives,
riding over huge wheels
looking for game and stories.

Early morning, he's gun-ready,
with birdshot for pheasants
safe from cataract-clouded eyes.

Smells of diesel fuel, dying
foliage, and coming snow
on October's air. He shouts:
    Let's go, dear girl!

6 AM Sunday Morning

Canada geese thick on the Beaver Pond.
Downy fuzz like froth at the shore,
swept from under their wings.
Everything's white this morning:
      fringes of hair on my father's head
      cataract film over his eyes
      the inside of our MacIntosh apples
      snow swirls around corn stalks
      our breath
      a sliver of moon

Night is hours away. Don't look for color.
Even home where flame under the pots
burns white. No flowers in an empty glass
vase, white gauzing through from the wall.

No matter. Our feet are dirt-black
on the walk home, nudging our blood red.

Another Spring
For Hope

On the hillside, loam pliant and ready:
ripple of fresh thunder,
branches burdened with sap.

My father comes from the house,
old and his heart weak. He wants
to plant maples with my daughter.

She lives in a small apartment in the Bronx,
a dancer finding her place, focused,
music in her bones like morning mist.

On the hillside their heads bend close,
hands joined over a root ball,
They send a troupe of seedlings across the hill.

Timing The Harvest

He moves through a field
of yellow canola grass.
Smells ready, he says.
White powdered shoes
from crushed butterflies,
so profuse they litter
ground around our footsteps.

Dark earth hardens and rebounds
after us in between the rows.
He takes a wide stance with armfuls
of hay, jack-hammers them
to make seeds fly, knows
their tumbling and drifting precisely.

He wants to go back to the house
where the world's best pie
is waiting for the farm-weary man.
Where lunch on the back porch
will only be for a few more days.
He admires his field, says:
           I love to watch things grow.

Inhalations

All night we heard air move though
his oxygen mask. Watched his chest
go up and down. Then one last time.

Removing the green elastic band,
I rub the line across Dad's temple—
a road across a field, an unnatural
marking, looping and going nowhere.

Outside, I inhale real air. I wish
he could have had his last breath
beneath a tree. Preferably maple.
Wind puffs through flowering crabs
and spring resists no more.

Ages Of The Barn

You halt at the last corner,
the shape of hills with their hold
on the season, an audience for geese.

You've walked this road,
cheeks blooming, with others
gathered close as if they were wings.

Over there, the unsuspecting barn
once stood like a formal gate,
red paint fading, tucked against the house.

Butternut beams, axe hewn,
walls with inscriptions from
handmade nails, dank manure smells.

And your father, always smiling,
worn hand on the barn door,
left ajar to let in air with its pulse of light.

In the silence, they have not forgotten you.
Here where you sit on the ground with another life
to live. Dead leaves falling in the dormant air.

Walking Past The Farm Where I Once Lived

The truck carrying Mom's things
up the hill spilled pots and bed boards—
items worth saving after Dad died.
The front door stood propped open.
No more worries about flies in the house.

By evening, we were finished
after weeks of discarding vacuums,
his neckties, broken chairs. Packing
her rolling pin, peonies, a trunk of letters,
she picked up her life and moved on.

Mother spent the last hour upstairs
alone in their bedroom. Slow as time,
she placed a hand on the stair wall.
Years to walk past as she came down,
her hand sliding over the rose-covered paper.

Goodbye old walls, she said
over and over. Her face a thin sheet.
Someone else owned this now.
That was among the best
lessons she ever gave me:

to hold the thoughts that carry you
down the stairs. Watch a leaf falling
in spirals even though winter is coming.
Love the house intricately patterned
with memory still rising into blue skies.

You Know Who

Now he's gone
she calls him—
You Know Who.

Geese coming in, the flag stiff
in a breeze. He's still around.
No need to speak his name.

East Meadow full of deer—
still safe, they move to her
window, wild-eyed and knowing.

Sweetie Pie

It will never be the same without my Sweetie Pie.
    Adeline to her daughter Nancy, September 28, 2000

The paper, a phone call maybe.
A banana for breakfast.
I might just tip back the chair for a nap.

Every day, men die
and women figure how to be alone
or they find an excuse to see doctors.
Some get used to a man
telling them what to do, where to go,
how to dress. Then, they're lost
and bake casseroles for the new widower.

Not me. Jim's gone. No more casseroles.
No kisses stolen in Ithaca or singing
"Bringing in the Sheaves" on New Year's Eve.

Sixty three years in the kitchen was enough—
hardly a moment, really, when you think of it.

Vanished

Geese are returning now.
Their black wings search for the Beaver
Pond—the address of wind and water.

One by one, they cry for companions
before night falls over the bare woods.
A moon rises beyond the bedroom window.

I feel alive in the half light. This is where home
calls and calls my name, past Mom's face
on the pillow, past today's vanished tracks.

My father's name sobs from her chest.
The bed shakes, her eyes screw shut, her body
curls in dementia. All day she could not speak.

I wonder about her words. I have no answers.
She clutches his pajama top like a child's blanket.
The sky full of signs and geometric proof of God.

Coda For Mom

In the long history of death,
yours seems one of the best
of worldly endings:
a June walk among peonies,
winged creatures feeding.
Later, a nap in the blue chair.
Sun-washed meadows.
Breath gone. Perfect stillness.

The Sap House

I step into the sap house. Sweet
steam of boiling sap infuses
the hut and soot darkened windows
become mirrors. A young girl of nine
sleeps near the warming pans.
Near the boiler, piles of wood
and tin buckets lean against the wall.
My father pulls at his pipe, tells
his boyhood stories for the assembled
children, ladles fresh syrup on cups
of new snow—Jack Wax. The winter day
shifts cold—weather for a good sap run.

The girl does not dream of me.

I walk out of the hut and she disappears
into summer's leafed maples and her next life.
In the dusk, fireflies begin to blink and I am
amazed at my love for her innocence.
Hundreds of lanterns search the dark.
Look! I will be the fireflies.

Beneath The Apple Trees
For Sarah

Either a thing will happen or it won't.
What I know as dependable is what I see
repeated: pink and white petals etch
the soft dirt in May's rain. Our footprints
in the mud fill with blossoms. Dark
branches weave against a sapphire sky
while wind strips petals, falling around us
                    like Brahms' notes.

Foundation

A crumbled road, dried up well,
hedgerows overgrown with wild
parsnip, and Queen Anne's lace
around an empty foundation.
Headstones of folks who lived here
coexist in the shade of maples.
No sugary smells or manure piles.
No hymns sung in farmhouse kitchens.
What doesn't move doesn't get attention.

My Father's Visit

Last night in the kitchen,
you were alive again, laughing
as I popped Sweet 100's
in my mouth. You smelled
of tobacco and gave advice
on growing tomatoes—
the importance of good dirt.

The Mower
For Debby

Fiddlehead ferns coil around graves
while grass, yellowed with dandelions,
yields to her mower blades. Each week,
in the summer, my sister spends a day
mowing the graveyard behind our church.
Her machine swerves around headstones
where friends and relatives are buried.

Their destinations of heaven or hell
unknown to her. Perhaps they still lie
astonished in their chambers, as she mows
among the ancestors and the newly dead.
She leaves fresh flowers for a forgotten
one, blows a kiss to grandmothers
whose stories we learned around our table.

Lengthy conversations with our parents
under their lids of earth mix with sweetness
of cut grass. She reads what's written
on headstones—wars fought, a child's life
shortened, Biblical quotes, marriages,
the last words. For a few hours, she listens
as they gather weightless and heard.

Feathers

Hope is the thing with feathers that perches in the soul.
     Emily Dickinson (254)

Atriums, valves, Purkinje fibers. My aorta sends
blood to the left ventricle, while I knead dough
against the wooden grain. *Lubb dupp, Lubb, dupp.*

A clock ticks on our pine mantle. Rain on a cedar roof.
Heart echoes infiltrate the kitchen. But what is in my heart
besides platelets and plasma rushing to their duties?

Egyptians believed the heart contained a vital essence
of the soul, and at death was weighed against feathers
to decide if a person went to Paradise. The lighter

the heart, the greater your chances. If so,
I am headed straight to Hell. But if hope
is in there too, my soul might have a chance—

my heart will beat against predictions, a perfect loaf
might emerge from the oven. In my kitchen, butter
and honey are ready. *Lubb dupp. Lubb dupp.*

Where The Words Are

Woman on the BART train—pearled ears,
gelled nails, bleached hair of the poet
thinking about her glass of wine when
she gets home. She moves her pen. A poem
forms like a segmented spinal column.

In the city, fog gathers on porches
of her children. Grown women.
The day stops speaking to her of their concerns.
She leans against the train window, thinks
of a life she might have lived.

So seamless is the transfer to another house,
a different climate. A place where geese come
in at night, forming and reforming overhead.
There are logs on a fire and Queen Anne's lace
on the mantle even in September.

She discards such solitude as a poem explodes
in the screech of metal. She writes with cool
air scripting scenes. Each word proclaims:
Here we are. We can bend. We can bend.
And in the dark window she sees her open eyes.

One Minute More

A man and a woman sit
after dinner, stare at sun's
reach over oak crusted hills,
the long light on green lawn.
They drink wine and talk
of those not seen in years,
of hope and not despair.
The dusk around them
holds itself taut, as robins
search for their evening meal.
Let's not go in yet, he begs.
        One minute more.

Notes

Notes From Her Journal, 1930, page 52:

I lift up mine eyes unto the hills, from whence cometh my help.
Psalm 121:1 (King's James Version)

In looking on the happy autumn fields,
and thinking of the days that are no more.
The Princess: Tears, Idle Tears
by Alfred, Lord Tennyson

Time, a maniac scattering dust,
And Life, a fury slinging flame.
Be Near Me When My Light Is Low
In Memoriam A. H. H. by Alfred, Lord Tennyson

Feathers, Epigraph, page 110:

Hope is the thing with feathers that perches in the soul.
by Emily Dickinson (254)

Poems by Alfred, Lord Tennyson and Emily Dickinson
are in the public domain.

Previously Published

Wedding Day: *Concho River Review*, December 2009

Ages of the Barn: *Blueline* Vol XXXVII 2016

Wind Still Blowing through Him: *Blueline* Vol XXXVII 2016

Millers Mills Ice Harvest: *Avocet, A Journal of Nature Poetry*,
October 2015

Feathers: San Mateo Poetry Contest Winner 2016

Feminine Geometry: *California Quarterly*, November 2018

The East End and The Mower: *Dandelion Review*, January
2018

In Appreciation

Deepest gratitude to my husband Larry for his love and support. This book would not be possible without him. Also to my extended family both past and present who who have loved and inspired me, and shared this heritage, especially my sisters, Susan, Debby, and Rebecca Hope, and my daughter Hope and her husband Matt, and daughter Sarah, and our three grandchildren.

Great thanks also to those in my poetry world—Eavan Boland, great friend and teacher; Robert Perry of Dutch Poet Press, phenomenal book designer and publisher; MJ Davey, whose great help made this book a reality; and my writer friends for years of thoughtful encouragement and poetry wisdom—Kara, Kelly, Netch, Narada, Brenda, Catherine, Nancy, Ross, Marylee, Stephanie, Erin, Suzanne, Jen, Lisa, Marian, Mary Lou, Rick, Veronica, and Ward.

About the Author

Nancy Huxtable Mohr was born a farmer's daughter, raised on Twin Pines, a two hundred-year-old family farm in Upstate New York. She graduated from Cornell University with a Bachelor of Science degree and has a California State Teacher's Credential. She now lives in Northern California with her husband Larry. She has worked in the arts both professionally and as a volunteer for 50 years. She has taught poetry in schools and a women's jail with California Poets in the Schools, and has published her poetry in literary journals. This is her first book.

Colophon

Cover and Interior Design by Robert Perry,
Dutch Poet Press and Robert Perry Book Design,
Palo Alto, California.

Printed and bound by IngramSpark.

Display and Text Typeface: Palatino